Understanding The Goals Of *9/11 As History*

Families and Work Institute has been privileged to work with Bank One to develop and distribute free Web-based tools for educators throughout the country as they continue to help children cope and contribute in a changing world.

The *9/11 As History* project grew out of our awareness that many educators wanted advice and assistance in helping children commemorate September 11 every year.

This book contains a brief summary of 16 unique lesson plans created for children from Pre-Kindergarten through the 12th grade. It also contains selections from the writings of children who responded to our invitation to share their thoughts and feelings about September 11. These selections reflect the full range of views and thoughts expressed, and are presented as young people wrote them (with their spelling, grammar and thoughts unchanged!).

THE GOALS OF *9/11 AS HISTORY*

When we entered into this partnership with Bank One to determine how to respond to educators' need for advice and assistance, our first task was to assemble an outstanding Advisory Board. This Advisory Board consisted of classroom teachers and school administrators (in locations both close to and far away from New York City, the District of Columbia, and Shanksville, Pennsylvania), child development experts, and educational experts. (For a list of the *9/11 As History* Advisory Board members, please see the Acknowledgements.)

As we discussed how best to develop classroom activities to commemorate September 11, we decided that the most important lessons to impart should focus on teaching the skills of DEMOCRACY. We were inspired by the words of Advisory Board member, Dr. Paul Houston, Executive Director, American Association of School Administrators. He noted that the 9/11 terrorists wanted to obliterate American values. We should, he said, help children understand what would be lost if American values were lost to the world. Fundamental among American values is our belief in democracy.

In addition, we were all committed to ensuring that the activities meet NATIONAL EDUCATIONAL STANDARDS.

With these premises in mind, we outlined the skills we thought were important to impart, searched for and then commissioned a number of well-known and well-respected groups and individuals to develop free, downloadable Web-based curricula for children in four age groups: Pre-Kindergarten-Grade 2, Grades 3-5, Grades 6-8, and Grades 9-12.

Taken together, these activities, emphasize democracy in the following ways:

Helping children feel safe. Without safety, there can be no learning. The writings of children scattered throughout this report reveal how frequently children's sense of safety was shattered. Thus, we have commissioned activities that help children of all ages find ways to feel safe.

Helping children understand heroism within themselves and others. It is important for children to understand heroism within others but also be inspired to see the heroic possibilities within us all. There are a number of activities that help children think about the heroes whom they meet every day and how they have the potential to be heroic themselves.

Helping children find and give support within their communities. The writings of children reveal that a common response to terrorism is to re-emphasize community—coming together and acting together. Our activities thus focus on building all kinds of supportive communities.

Helping children learn perspective-taking. Research on children's development reveals that being able to understand the perspectives of others is an important foundation for emotional, social, and cognitive learning and is a strong antidote to gratuitous violence. This skill is different from tolerance because it doesn't necessarily mean accepting intentionally harmful (or good) actions of others. It means that children gain a perspective on why people behave in the ways they do as a prelude to judgment and action. A number of the *9/11 As History* activities provide opportunities for children to practice the skill of perspective-taking.

Helping children become critical thinkers. Fundamental to democracy are informed and engaged citizens. We provide activities that help children evaluate complex issues and different points of view.

Helping children understand the historical antecedents of terrorism.
High-school students are ready to learn about terrorism in the past and in
the present, so we commissioned some activities that explore this issue.

Helping children identify and respect American values. Key to all of
these lessons is identifying the values that are most important to our
country and respecting these American values.

THE RESPONSE TO 9/11 AS HISTORY

Since their release in 2002, the response to the *9/11 As History* curricula
and materials has been overwhelmingly positive. Our Web site,
www.911AsHistory.org, and the initiative were featured in *The New York
Times, American Teacher, NEA Today, The Los Angeles Times, The
Chicago Tribune,* and *The Washington Post,* among others. In addition,
entire school districts, including Dallas, Texas and Phoenix, Arizona
adopted the curricula for their teachers to use in commemorating the first
anniversary of September 11 with students.

In the months following last September 11, there have been many
other events (such as the war in Iraq, the sniper attacks, and the crash
of the space shuttle) that have caused children to ask questions and
educators to consider how best to answer them. Although these materials
were designed to commemorate September 11, educators around the
country have told us that these materials have also been very useful in
these and other situations.

We hope that you will find this resource valuable in your own classroom, and that you will let other educators know about this resource as
they too, look for ways to help children cope and contribute in our ever-
changing world.

Ellen Galinsky
President, Families and Work Institute
July, 2003

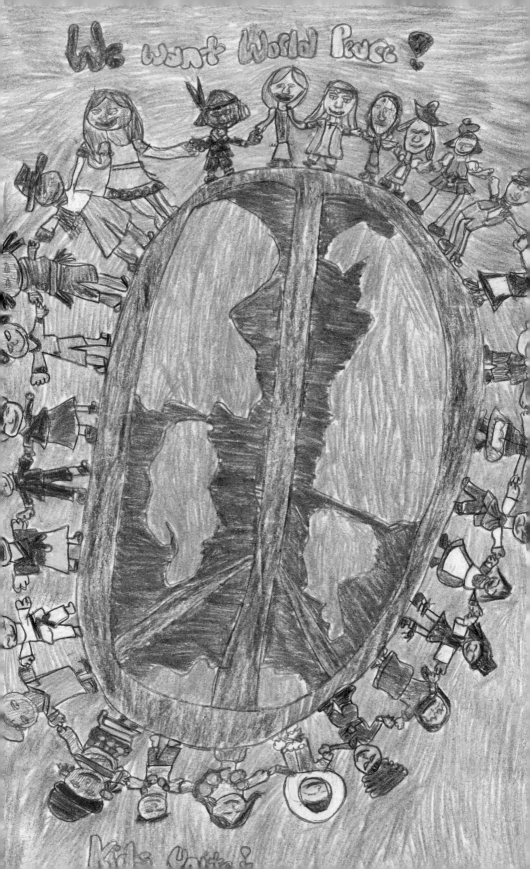

TABLE OF CONTENTS

FOREWORD

September 11, 2001, was a day of horrific tragedy and sorrow for our nation and the world. It was also a day that America came together as one in support of our country and its people. Individuals throughout the United States yearned to help in any way they could. Here at Bank One, our employees raised nearly $1.5 million in just two weeks. That money was matched by the Bank One Foundation and then donated to a number of organizations serving victims of the tragedy.

Although most of Bank One's contributions went to organizations that were either assisting families who had lost relatives or helping small businesses that were shattered, we also made a grant to the Families and Work Institute that has proved to be extraordinarily important. The Institute focused its efforts on helping America's young people cope with, and even learn from, the events of September 11.

Working with a panel of leading educators, the Families and Work Institute tackled the many issues that arose from the events of September 11, issues such as the meaning of heroism and patriotism, the impact of the media on the way we think, and how to cope with reactions such as fear, loss, and perhaps even racist thoughts. These are all issues we struggle with as adults, but the effect they have on our children can be even more profound. Educators and parents knew they needed to help our children work through these concerns, but in the days following the tragedy it seemed that nothing could truly prepare us for the task. How could we begin to explain something that we, as adults, found so difficult to comprehend?

With these thoughts in mind, the Families and Work Institute began work in the spring of 2002 to develop age-appropriate curricula that would help children cope with the tragedy. They had a sense of urgency that was driven by the realization that the first anniversary of September 11 would coincide with the opening weeks of school, giving teachers little time to prepare lesson plans. That meant working fast to create world-class curricula that school districts could get into the classroom on day one.

The team was committed to meeting what seemed to be an unrealistic deadline. Using the Internet, the Institute was able to distribute lesson plans to every school just as teachers were returning to their classrooms.

The response from teachers, children, and parents has been tremendous. We have all come to realize, however, that the work is just beginning. As the discussion of September 11 moves from "current events" to "history," teachers and students will continue to need a support system to help them work through the feelings that will inevitably arise on each anniversary of that tragic day.

All of us at Bank One are grateful to the staff at the Families and Work Institute for their hard work and dedication to this project. We join with the Institute in saluting the educators, administrators, and historians who came together to help create such a comprehensive educational program. Most important, however, we want to thank the thousands of teachers across this country who have taken the time to work with their children on these lessons. These are difficult topics, and it takes personal strength to help children address them. The teachers' personal dedication will help ensure that our nation's children emerge from this tragedy stronger and more committed than ever to the values that make this country great.

Jamie Dimon
Chairman and Chief Executive Officer
Bank One

I am still the same me I was on September 10th, with just an added experience to my life. Honestly, I think more than anything the whole event has confused me. I don't understand so much. I don't understand how people could feel what ever they felt and do

Girl, Age 14, 9th Grade
Alameda, CA
September 10, 2002

something so terrible. I don't understand all these feelings I'm 'supposed' to feel that are being shoved down my throat. I don't understand the feelings I actually do have about the events of 9/11 because everyone else's feelings have influenced me so much.

In a way, I'm scared, but you have to be scared before you can be brave. I used to not think about biological warfare, terrorist invasions, and things like that because, I believe that that kind of stuff didn't really exist in America, it doesn't happen in America. Now I do worry, but I think that it has been good for me because it opened my eyes to what is happening everyday in some places.

Girl, Age 12, 8th Grade
Savannah, GA
September 10, 2002

When most people hear September 11, 2001
they would think of the world trade centers.
WELL, I think of those too, but I also think of the plane
that crashed in Pennsylvania.

If those brave people on the plane hadn't made
that attempt to kill the hi-jacker the plane
would have crashed in the white house.
If that plane had crashed into the white house,
we could be without a president as we speak.

I hope that the people who died on the Pennsylvania plane,
knew they were going to die as heroes.

GIRL, AGE 14, 8TH GRADE
SUDBURY, MA
SEPTEMBER 11, 2002

It has given me more reason to accomplish the goals I have set for myself. One example is the fact that I want to defend my country as a soldier, September 11 has instilled a burst of energy in me to want to do my all to help the country. The peoples lives that were lost has given me a reason to prove that we must all help one another in anyway possible.

Girl, Age 17, 12th Grade, Chicago, IL, September 11, 2002

All Kinds of Feelings

Anti-Defamation League

Theme covered:
Helping Children Learn Perspective-Taking

Overview of activity:
How can those who teach and care for young children help them learn to
identify their own and others' feelings and emotions? This activity provides
an opportunity to assist children in creatively exploring feelings through
reflection, discussion, art, and movement.

- Students are asked to bring magazines into their program. Educators ask
  children to look through the magazines and talk about the emotions they
  see in the illustrations. This discussion then invites children to reflect on
  their own feelings about starting a new school year, meeting new children
  and teachers, and experiencing new environments. Educators work with
  children to create a class collage—a visual representation of feelings to use
  as a catalyst for discussions throughout the year. Students and educators
  may also discuss and act out how body language can express emotion.

Objectives of activity:
Students will:
- reflect on, explore, and share their feelings;
- learn about the connection between words, actions and feelings;
- create visual representations to depict a variety of feelings; and
- develop empathy for other children through sharing personal experiences
  and exploring commonly-shared emotions and feelings.

Subjects with which this lesson interfaces:
Language Arts, Art, Dance/Movement

Estimated time of activity:
One to three class meetings (approximately 20 minutes each)

National educational standards that this lesson meets:
- Head Start Child Outcomes: Standards for Language
- Head Start Child Outcomes: Standards for Creative Arts
- Head Start Child Outcomes: Standards for Social
  and Emotional Development
- Head Start Child Outcomes: Standards for Physical Health
  and Development
- McRel: Standards for Language Arts
- McRel: Standards for Thinking and Reasoning
- McRel: Standards for Health
- McRel: Standards for Art Connection
- McRel: Standards for Visual Arts
- McRel: Standards for Dance
- McRel: Standards for Working with Others

** This complete lesson plan is available for free at www.911AsHistory.org.
The "All Kinds of Feelings" lesson plan, including a list of required materials
and detailed teaching procedure with assessment recommendations and
extended activities, downloads as a 13-page document.

Everyday Heroes

Reading Rainbow

Theme covered:
Helping Children Understand Heroism within Themselves and Others

Overview of activity:
Using the book *Max* by Bob Graham and the accompanying Reading Rainbow video as springboards for discussion, students identify the heroes in their everyday lives and discuss the attributes and deeds that make these individuals heroic.

- In the first lesson, educators begin by asking students to define what a hero is and to name heroes whom they know of. Answers are written on a blackboard or chart. If students name fictional heroes along with people or occupations from everyday life, educators can use this opportunity to discuss the difference between heroes on television or in the movies (some of whom might be "superheroes") and real-life, everyday heroes. Students are then directed to look for all kinds of heroes as they watch the video program. After viewing, they name additional kinds of heroes they noticed in the program and add them to the chart.

- In the second lesson, educators lead students in composing and editing a class poem about heroes that includes the qualities of heroes. The poem is bound in a book.

- In a follow-up activity, educators may discuss with students the idea that not all heroes are famous, nor do all heroic activities make the news. Sometimes our heroes are at home or in our classrooms, and often the heroic deeds are acts of kindness, helpfulness, and generosity. Students are encouraged to look for heroes who are nearby. It is suggested that educators regularly hold discussions about these heroes and what they do that makes them heroic.

Objectives of activity:
Students will:
- be able to define a "hero" and identify heroes in their everyday lives by discussing the qualities and deeds that make a person "heroic;" and
- demonstrate their understanding of the concept of "heroes" by contributing to a class-composed poem.

Subjects with which this lesson interfaces:
Social Studies, Language Arts

Estimated time of activity:
Two class periods
- Day 1: 25 minutes (to view Reading Rainbow video), plus 5 minutes for pre-viewing discussion and 5 minutes for post-viewing discussion
- Day 2: 20 minutes as a group, plus individual time for illustrating

National educational standards that this lesson meets:
- NCSS: Standards for Social Studies
- National Council of Teachers of English and the International Reading Association: Standards for Language Arts

** This complete lesson plan is available for free at www.911AsHistory.org. The "Everyday Heroes" lesson plan, including a list of required materials and detailed teaching procedure with assessment recommendations and extended activities, downloads as a 7-page document.

Help Them Feel Safe

Virginia Kimball, Volunteer for The American Red Cross

Theme covered:
Helping Children Feel Safe

Overview of activity:
This activity provides young children with two lessons to help them feel safe.
- The first lesson encourages children to identify and then to make stick puppets of the community professionals who are responsible for keeping people safe and conduct a puppet show to role-play how these professionals would respond to various situations. In putting on the puppet show, students form teams that work together, as another demonstration of what community helpers do. Educators ask leading questions or pose problems to help the students clarify roles. For example, they may ask, "What happens when a building catches fire? How does the fire department find out about it? If you are the firefighter, what is your job?"
- The second lesson encourages students to share what they are feeling during times of crisis as well as in everyday situations. Educators should listen carefully and observe children's body language to help them name their feelings. Students brainstorm words that suggest feelings and listen to a story that teaches that an important thing about feelings is that they can change.

Objectives of activity:
Students will:
- identify community helpers who work to keep people safe;
- identify a range of personal feelings; and
- recognize and be responsive to others' feelings.

Subjects with which this lesson interfaces:
History, Health, Language Arts, Working with Others

Estimated time of activity:
Two 20-30 minute blocks

National educational standards that this lesson meets:
• McRel: Standards for History
• McRel: Standards for Health
• McRel: Standards for Language Arts
• McRel: Standards for Working with Others

** This complete lesson plan is available for free at www.911AsHistory.org. The "Help Them Feel Safe" lesson plan, including a list of required materials and detailed teaching procedure with assessment recommendations and extended activities, downloads as a 6-page document.

What's Special About Me?

Families GOALS Project; Maureen Underwood,
LCSW, Coordinator

Theme covered:
Helping Children Feel Safe

Overview of activity:
This curriculum is built upon research with children that reveals the importance of "protective factors" in providing resistance to risk as well as promote patterns of adaptation and coping. Using a creative activity as a medium, this lesson helps children identify factors that can help them respond constructively to stress. The factors include having a positive sense of self and having a positive and enduring relationship with at least one significant adult with whom the child identifies.

- Students are given a body outline and asked to draw the parts of themselves they like the best. Emphasis is on normal body parts that make them individual, unique and special. Students are asked to share their thoughts about their drawings with the class after they are completed. When the sharing is completed, students are reminded that each of them has at least one special person in their life who truly appreciates what a talented and important person they are. Students are asked to identify that person and share with the class why they have chosen him or her. Students are then invited to give their picture of themselves to that special person.

Objectives of activity:
Students will:
- introduce the concept of self-affirmation; and
- identify a supportive adult in their environment.

Subjects with which this lesson interfaces:
Art

Estimated time of activity:
One class period

National educational standards that this lesson meets:
- McRel: Standards for Self-Regulation

** This complete lesson plan is available for free at www.911AsHistory.org. The "What's Special about Me?" lesson plan, including a list of required materials and detailed teaching procedure with assessment recommendations and extended activities, downloads as a 5-page document.

After it happened,

instead of people creating panic,

going nuts,or turning their backs on each other, people

become more considerate.

Even strangers

were helping each other.

This made me feel better because when it happened I

thought the world was going to go crazy and it didn't.

It did exactly the opposite.

Girl, Age 12, 7th Grade, Anacoco, LA, September 12, 2002

Unity is an i
thing in a co
shouldn't dis
hate. You sho
everyone. Th
make a comm
Otherwise, yo
people living

Girl, Age 14, 9th Grade, Tallahassee, FL, September 11, 2002

portant

munity, we

riminate or

uld love

t is what

unity.

u are just

n a place.

It's made me look at my mother as a hero, because she's a firefighter.

Girl, Age 15, 11th Grade
Casa Grande, AZ
September 3, 2002

I have yet to travel on a plane since that day and don't know when I will travel on one again. I admit that even with all the security now that I am scared of flying. I never had a fear of flying until that horrific day of September 11th, the day that 3000 souls cried.

Boy, Age 17, 12th Grade, Chicago, IL
September 11, 2002

GRADE 3 THROUGH GRADE 5

Heroes in Real Life

Virginia Kimball, Volunteer for The American Red Cross

Themes covered:
Helping Children Understand Heroism within Themselves and Others
Helping Children Identify and Respect American Values

Overview of activity:
These activities help students describe the nature of a hero and recognize
the differences between real-life heroes and fictional heroes. Students also
focus on their personal heroes and have an opportunity to share information
about them.

- In the first lesson, educators lead a discussion to define the actions and
  qualities that make a person a hero or heroine, listing these character
  traits for the entire class to see. Educators and students then make com-
  parisons between superheroes or fictional heroes and real-life heroes. The
  students create posters using images and words to show the differences
  between these two types of heroes and share their understanding of the
  distinction between reality and fantasy. The first class period concludes
  with a discussion about how heroes contribute to one's community and
  country and about what it takes to be an everyday hero.
- The second lesson continues the previous class period's discussion about
  heroic qualities and actions. Educators introduce the concept of the
  "unsung hero" to the students and together brainstorm examples of this
  particular type of hero. In the next activity, the students identify their own
  personal hero through an essay assignment and a portrait (using collage
  or drawing materials) that utilize symbols of their hero's behavior or
  characteristics. At the end of class, each student tells the class about
  their hero and posts their portrait.

Objectives of activity:
Students will:
- identify and analyze the qualities and actions of heroes;
- compare and contrast heroes and superheroes;
- describe their personal hero; and
- discover that anyone can be a hero.

Subjects with which this lesson interfaces:
History, Civics, Language Arts

Estimated time of activity:
One to two class periods plus time for individual presentations

National educational standards that this lesson meets:
- McRel: Standards for History
- McRel: Standards for Civics
- McRel: Standards for Language Arts

** This complete lesson plan is available for free at www.911AsHistory.org. The "Heroes in Real Life" lesson plan, including a list of required materials and detailed teaching procedure with assessment recommendations and extended activities, downloads as a 7-page document.

Looking At the World Through Different Eyes

Families GOALS Project; Maureen Underwood, LCSW, Coordinator

Themes covered:
Helping Children Learn Perspective-Taking
Helping Children Understand Heroism within Themselves and Others

Overview of activity:
Using a short story to stimulate classroom discussion, this lesson employs metaphor to depict an incident evoking September 11. This activity teaches children the technique of cognitive restructuring to suggest that even terrible situations can be seen through a different point of view.
• This activity includes the original short story, *The Snow Globe*, in its entirety. The story is read to the class and a discussion follows. The discussion questions encourage students to think about negative situations from a variety of perspectives and to appreciate the value of adults in one's support system. The questions also ask the students to put themselves into the story and reflect on their own feelings.

Objectives of activity:
Students will:
• learn reframing as a problem-solving alternative; and
• identify an issue in their own lives that they would like to be able to view in a more positive way.

Subjects with which this lesson interfaces:
Science, English

Estimated time of activity:
One class period, with potential for extension into several additional class sessions

National educational standards that this lesson meets:
• McRel: Standard of Self-Regulation

** This complete lesson plan is available for free at www.911AsHistory.org. The "Looking at the World through Different Eyes" lesson plan, including a list of required materials and detailed teaching procedure with assessment recommendations and extended activities, downloads as an 8-page document.

Stitching Together a Community

Anti-Defamation League

Theme covered:
Helping Children Learn Perspective-Taking

Overview of activity:
The *Stitching Together a Community* activity encourages students, through a variety of reflective and interactive processes, to think about community on both a local and national level, and to consider the many ways community can be defined and the ways in which their diverse communities provide support, strength, and pride.

- In the first lesson, educators begin by asking students to help generate a list of the different kinds of communities to which they belong. Educators can tell students that communities often develop because they are unified by certain common elements: language, geography, family relationships, religion, interests such as sports teams, etc. Educators then ask students to think about communities they are a part of and point out that most people can belong to more than one community.
- In the second lesson, students each have an opportunity to design and create quilt squares to represent what is important to them about at least two of their own communities. Once the quilt squares are completed, they are joined together (stitched or taped or tied with strings depending on the material used) to make a classroom community quilt. This activity provides a way for students to share their own stories or traditions about their communities with their classmates.
- In the third lesson, students sit in a circle and lay the quilt squares out in the middle. Educators suggest that everyone take a few minutes to look at all the quilt squares and marvel at their colorful diversity and unique designs. Educators encourage students to explain the meaning of their designs to each other.

Objectives of activity:
Students will:
- develop an understanding of the various communities to which they belong, including the United States of America;
- develop an appreciation of the support, especially in difficult times, that communities can provide;
- gain an understanding of and respect for their own and others' communities; and
- practice listening and empathy skills as they share their own and learn about others' perspectives about diverse communities.

Subjects with which this lesson interfaces:
Social Studies, Language Arts, Art

Estimated time of activity:
Three 45-60 minute class periods

National educational standards that this lesson meets:
- NCSS: Standards of Excellence
- NCTE: Standards for the Language Arts

** This complete lesson plan is available for free at www.911AsHistory.org. The "Stitching Together a Community" lesson plan, including a list of required materials and detailed teaching procedure with assessment recommendations and extended activities, downloads as a 7-page document.

Yes, I Can

Robin Gurwitch, PhD,
University of Oklahoma Health Sciences Center

Themes covered:
Helping Children Feel Safe
Helping Children Understand Heroism within Themselves and Others

Overview of activity:
A common response to a traumatic event in children is fear coupled with a diminished sense of safety. These strong emotions can impact a child's ability to learn. This lesson plan is designed to help children identify and confront fear in a positive manner.

- In the first lesson, children read a book titled *Jumping Into Nothing* to introduce them to the theme of facing one's fears. The class has an opportunity to share some specific things that may make someone afraid and to connect those with possible physiological reactions to fears. The discussion then moves into practical ways that students can address their fears, including talking with someone, asking for help or singing songs (e.g. "My Favorite Things"). The students continue by making a poster listing the people in their lives to whom they can talk about their fears and the people in their communities whose job it is to keep them safe.
- In the second lesson, educators and students review the previous class period's discussion about fears and safety. The emphasis of this discussion is on how being afraid is a normal reaction to certain events, but how these fears can be overcome. Students make individual collages from magazine clippings to show the things they can also do instead of feeling afraid or to help others in times of worry and fear.

Objectives of activity:
Students will:
- identify specific fears and physiological reactions;
- discuss ways to address or overcome those fears; and
- pinpoint the people in their lives that can help them with their fears.

Subjects with which this lesson interfaces:
Art, Music, Health, and Social Studies

Estimated time of activity:
Two class periods

National educational standards that this lesson meets:
• McRel: Standards of Health
• Capstone-Press: Standards of Health
• NCSS: Standards for Social Studies
• McRel: Standards for Visual Arts
• McRel: Standards for Music
• McRel: Standards for Life Skills

** This complete lesson plan is available for free at www.911AsHistory.org.
The "Yes, I Can" lesson plan, including a list of required materials and
detailed teaching procedure with assessment recommendations and extended
activities, downloads as a 7-page document.

Getting over prejudices is the most important thing our country can do, it will improve morale a lot. Different religions and races are often feuding, but it seems like there isn't a point to all this.

Boy, Age 13, 8th Grade
Little Rock, AR
September 9, 2002

I've lived in my community almost my whole life. I don't personally have a community, no one talks to each other. They all kinda just keep to themselves, and don't really communicate. The only thing that I've personally seen is the American Flag being hung up all over. I couldn't do anything cause honestly I'm to shy to make a difference.

It made me realize all the illness, in the world around us as well as within the united states, and from this awareness I became more interested in international relations and world view's, I began to pay more attention to the new's and I'm concerned about the event's that are taking place in our fragile world and how they affect us as a country.

Girl, Age 18, 12th Grade, Laguna Beach, CA, November 22, 2002

There are people who want to leave children as parentless, husbands and wives as widows, friends without their companion and parents without children. I have had to accept that America is not as safe as I thought it was, but I have also learned that it can be as safe as we make it.

Girl, Age 14, 9th Grade, Kingsville, TX, September 12, 2002

34

Analyzing Messages in Popular Culture

Educators for Social Responsibility

Themes covered:
Helping Children Become Critical Thinkers
Helping Children Identify and Respect American Values

Overview of activity:
These activities encourage students to examine persuasive techniques used in the media and help them differentiate between what others believe and their own values and beliefs.
- In the first lesson, students identify different values that characters express in a Dr. Seuss book for the purpose of understanding different points of view. Educators help students explore that many messages use persuasive techniques. Students begin to share and identify opinion versus fact with the use of the words, "I think," "I feel," and "I believe." Students are asked to identify persuasive techniques and messages that are used in our culture.
- In the second lesson, students listen to age-appropriate popular songs while reading the lyrics. Educators break students up into smaller groups and help students examine persuasive techniques used in the songs, determine what messages or beliefs were intended for the listener, and whether they agree or disagree with them. Educators facilitate a group conversation, encouraging students to assess their own values and positions as they encounter and process information.

Objectives of activity:
Students will:
- recognize persuasive techniques;
- think critically about the messages contained in various media;
- discuss controversial issues in constructive ways; and
- analyze the deeper messages contained in children's literature and popular songs.

Subjects with which this lesson interfaces:
English, Language Arts, Social Studies, History, Civics, Music

Estimated time of activity:
Two 40-50 minute class periods

National educational standards that this lesson meets:
• McRel: Standards for Language Arts
• McRel: Standards for Civics
• McRel: Standards for World History
• McRel: Standards for Music

** This complete lesson plan is available for free at www.911AsHistory.org.
The "Analyzing Messages in Popular Culture" lesson plan, including a list of
required materials and detailed teaching procedure with assessment recommendations and extended activities, downloads as a 13-page document.

Building Strength Through Knowledge

Robin H. Gurwitch, PhD,
University of Oklahoma Health Sciences Center

Themes covered:
Helping Children Become Critical Thinkers
Helping Children Feel Safe

Overview of activity:
In the aftermath of a traumatic event, children typically experience increased fears and worries about their own safety and security. These reactions, and others, can adversely impact children's ability to concentrate in school, and impair their learning potential. Such emotions can be exacerbated through information presented in the media.

- In the first lesson, educators and students discuss the wide range of feelings that people can experience in response to different kinds of events. Students write out the emotions that they encountered following the tragic events of September 11 as well as following positive events in their lives. Educators help students think of ways that fears and worries can be diminished and generate lists of groups or individuals who can help them do so. Educators introduce the idea that the media can also affect our emotions and attitudes about events. Students are given an assignment to review media coverage from September 11 and record the emotions and attitudes the material was trying to generate.

- In the second lesson, students review differences between fact and opinion. Using examples from the September 11 media coverage students reviewed, they identify the underlying goals in presenting these news stories. The students look at different historical events and how the media used fact and opinion to influence general feelings and attitudes about these events. These activities help students become critical thinkers, a fundamental skill in a democratic society.

Objectives of activity:
Students will:
- better understand what role the media can play in our emotions;
- learn skills to address negative feelings;
- critically examine media information; and
- enhance their resiliency skills to better manage problems that can arise.

Subjects with which this lesson interfaces:
Health, Life Skills, Language Arts, History, and Social Studies

Estimated time of activity:
Two to three class periods/meetings (plus additional homework)

National educational standards that this lesson meets:
- McRel: Standards for Health
- Capstone-Press: Standards for Health
- NCSS: Standards for Social Studies
- McRel: Standards for History
- McRel: Standards for Language Arts
- NCTE: Standards for Language Arts
- McRel: Standards for Life Skills

** This complete lesson plan is available for free at www.911AsHistory.org.
The "Building Strength through Knowledge" lesson plan, including a list of
required materials and detailed teaching procedure with assessment recommendations and extended activities, downloads as an 8-page document.

Community Citizens, Community Banner

Do Something, Inc.

Themes covered:
Helping Children Identify and Respect American Values
Helping Children Become Critical Thinkers

Overview of activity:
In this lesson, students learn the history and symbolism of flags and reflect on how flags represent their community and nation.

- The first lesson begins by exploring the history of flags, specifically the American flag and students' state flag. Students discuss what it means to be an American today after the experiences of September 11. The qualities and values they identify become the basis for community banners that the students create in small groups. Students are assigned to gather responses from family, friends and other members of the community about what being an American today means to them to bring to the next class period.
- The second lesson continues the discussion about being an American. Students share the responses that they gathered from others. Working in small groups, they design their own community banners using various art materials. These banners reflect some of the ideals that were generated from the previous discussions. An event may also be organized to present the banners to the school and/or community.

Objectives of activity:
Students will:
- develop a deeper understanding and appreciation of the values that shape them and their communities;
- explore what it means to be a "citizen" in the community in the wake of September 11; and
- learn about the history of the United States and/or their state flag.

Subjects with which this lesson interfaces:
History, English, Language Arts, Civics, Social Studies

Estimated time of activity:
One to two class periods (plus additional homework assignment)

National educational standards that this lesson meets:
- McRel: Standards for Civics
- McRel: Standards for History
- McRel: Standards for Language Arts

** This complete lesson plan is available for free at www.911AsHistory.org. The "Community Citizens, Community Banner" lesson plan, including a list of required materials and detailed teaching procedure with assessment recommendations and extended activities, downloads as a 10-page document.

Examining and Interrupting Hate

Anti-Defamation League

Themes covered:
Helping Children Become Critical Thinkers
Helping Children Learn Perspective-Taking

Overview of activity:
This lesson provides an opportunity for students to develop a vocabulary and understanding of potentially unfair and hateful attitudes and behaviors.
- In the first lesson, students define the terms stereotyping, prejudice, discrimination and scapegoating. They think about the meaning of the words, generate examples that illustrate each term and consider the potential consequences of these examples. Educators then provide a series of statements for the students to use in practicing the identification of these concepts.
- In the second lesson, the students use a pyramid diagram of the four terms and create examples to illustrate how negative attitudes and behaviors can escalate. The students then focus their examples on Arab Americans and how the events of September 11 led to stereotypes, prejudice, discrimination and scapegoating of this group. After the small groups have shared their examples with the class, there is a whole-group discussion to review the lesson and consider ways for individuals to stop the escalation of hatred.

Objectives of activity:
Students will:
- explore the concepts of stereotyping, prejudice, discrimination, and scapegoating;
- consider how the events of September 11 have led to stereotyping, prejudice, discrimination, and scapegoating of Arab Americans and others; and
- identify ways that they can interrupt the escalation of hatred in their schools and communities and consider the value of taking such actions.

Subjects with which this lesson interfaces:
Current Events, Social Studies, U.S. History

Estimated time of activity:
Two to three class periods

National educational standards that this lesson meets:
• National Center for History in the Schools: Standards for U.S. History

** This complete lesson plan is available for free at www.911AsHistory.org. The "Examining and Interrupting Hate" lesson plan, including a list of required materials and detailed teaching procedure with assessment recommendations and extended activities, downloads as a 9-page document.

The next time you see someone on your street don't just say well they don't dress like I do or they don't look like a person I would hang out with. **You never know** The person right next door might turn to be the nicest person you have ever met. Just take five minutes to get to know the person. That's all you have to do you don't have to be there best friend. **Just talking** to them might make their day that much better.

Girl, Age 14, 8th Grade

Glenbrook, NV

September 11, 2002

The events of September 11, 2001
have changed me in a very big way.
I feel weird knowing that someday I
will be telling my kids and grandkids
about that tragic day, just like my
grandparents have told me about
World War II and other tragic events
in history.

Boy, Age 16, 11th Grade
Marble Hill, MO
September 11, 2002

Many people say that September 11th changed the world. I, however, do not believe this. September 11th was the day America woke up to the rest of the world. It was the day we realized we were not isolated from the troubles of humanity.

Do you not believe me? Whose lives were changed when the U.S. embassies were terrorized in Tanzania and Kenya? Who had a renewed interest in religion after the U.S.S. Cole was attacked. These events did not change our world. We live in a bubble of national- ism. That very nationalistic pride in which we hide behind, the very arrogance in which we are known throughout the world keeps us from true understanding.

Boy, Age 16, 11th Grade, Casa Grande, AZ, September 3, 2002

Diversity: Our Strength— Our Challenge

Anti-Defamation League

Themes covered:
Helping Children Learn Perspective-Taking
Helping Children Identify and Respect American Values

Overview of activity:
On September 11, 2001 Americans were the targets of hatred. This highly interactive three-part lesson creates a supportive forum for students to explore the dynamics of hateful behavior and the strength of unified action to counter it.

- In the first lesson, students draw symbols that personally characterize aspects of their own lives, such as gender, race, ethnicity, religion, and citizenship. Educators facilitate students in sharing their symbols and engage them in conversation posing the following questions:
    - Do people see each other clearly?
    - What influences affect perception of other people and events?
- In the second lesson, using the characteristics identified by students previously, educators conduct an exercise to illustrate the concepts of similarities and differences. Students are asked to consider when they feel alone or part of the majority and how these emotions affect each of them personally, in relation to feeling targeted, included or excluded.
- The third lesson calls on students to observe incidents of bias and or name-calling in their own environments, and discuss how they feel when witnessing these acts. Students break up into small groups and work on an exercise called "Roles People Play," evaluating the consequences of interrupting or remaining bystanders when they see acts of bias occur. Educators share strategies to confront bias, and elicit additional strategies from students.

Objectives of activity:

Students will:

- depict and share important influences that have shaped their own cultural, religious, gender and social beliefs;
- share their own and learn of others' personal experiences with prejudice;
- examine the roles that each person plays in either perpetuating or interrupting prejudice and bias; and
- learn effective strategies to confront bias.

Subjects with which this lesson interfaces:

Civics, English, Language Arts, Sociology, Social Studies

Estimated time of activity:

Two to three class periods

National educational standards that this lesson meets:

- McRel: Standards for Behavioral Studies
- McRel: Standards for Civics
- McRel: Standards for Working with Others

** This complete lesson plan is available for free at www.911AsHistory.org. The "Diversity: Our Strength—Our Challenge" lesson plan, including a list of required materials and detailed teaching procedure with assessment recommendations and extended activities, downloads as a 13-page document.

Exploring 9/11 in Historical, Cultural and International Context: "Why Here, Why Us, Why Now?"

James McGrath Morris, West Springfield High School and Kathleen Anderson Steeves, PhD, George Washington University

Themes covered:
Helping Children Understand the Historical Antecedents of Terrorism
Helping Children Become Critical Thinkers

Overview of activity:
Like most international conflicts, the root causes of September 11 go far back in history and are themselves a lesson in how actions taken in the past affect us today.

- The first part of this unit (three lessons lasting approximately 90 minutes each) asks students to trace the similarities and differences among the three major religions in Western history—Judaism, Christianity, and Islam—and make connections to the events of September 11. Educators provide students with a substantial list of resources to research and investigate the historical development of major religions and answer questions posed within the lesson plan. Students have the opportunity to work in small groups and display and share their work. Educators facilitate students' understanding of the historical connections among these three major religions and the economic and political factors that have continued to make the interactions of these religions important in the world today.

- In the second lesson, students examine surveys of public opinion in other nations and identify reasons, factors, and events that have shaped, and continue to shape, these attitudes. Educators divide students into groups, each representing a geographic section of the world. Students are asked to research and explore data reflecting perceptions of the United States. Findings are presented to the class and educators facilitate discussion on the data and their implications for the United States, a perspective that is important in the increasingly global context in which they live.

- The third lesson enables students to compare the attacks on the United States on September 11 with other human-induced calamitous events in history and examine whether technological change in communications, transportation, and weaponry have altered terrorism. Students are asked to research at least three attacks on the United States (aside from September 11) and analyze whether the attacks on September 11 were unprecedented. Students with similar points of view will pair up, and the educators facilitate discussions with students who have opposing points of view.
- Additionally, this unit includes two extensions that educators may use as part of the lessons or as stand-alone activities. The first enables students to consider a longer historical view of the attacks and consider how images are used in shaping and commemorating seminal events in history. The second examines the issue of war-making in the American government, focusing specifically on the War Powers Act of 1973.

Objectives of activity:
Students will:
- recognize and describe the basic ideas of the three religions;
- use maps to identify the spread of the religions and location of that growth;
- develop a visual display to describe the relationships among the three major religions over time;
- recognize how events in the centuries-old conflict between the three major religions of the West are connected to the attack on the United States in 2001;
- draw conclusions from data and create hypotheses;
- identify how people in different parts of the world view the United States and explore reasons for the divergent views;
- develop policy ideas that might alter views of the United States' position in the world;
- place the events of September 11 in context with other attacks and evaluate their historical significance; and
- apply evidentiary skills and analysis.

Subjects with which this lesson interfaces:
History, Civics, Government, English, Language Arts (portions), Geography (portions)

Estimated time of activity:
The entire unit would require a minimum of three blocks of time (90 minutes each), but would more likely fill four blocks. Each portion of the unit, however, can be taught as a single lesson. Additionally, each lesson can easily be modified due to time constraints and the abilities of students.

National educational standards that this lesson meets:
• McRel: Standards for Civics
• McRel: Standards for History
• McRel: Standards for Language Arts

** This complete lesson plan is available for free at www.911AsHistory.org. The "Exploring September 11 in Historical, Cultural and International Context: 'Why Here, Why Us, Why Now?'" lesson plan, including a list of required materials and detailed teaching procedure with assessment recommendations and extended activities, downloads as a 29-page document.

Re-Examining Democracy in a Post September 11 World

Lotika Shaunik Paintal, Director, Post September 11 Education Consortium

Themes covered:
Helping Children Identify and Respect American Values
Helping Children Learn Perspective-Taking

Overview of activity:
This lesson plan seeks to inform and actively involve high school students in current events, to engage them in democratic processes, and to include their voices and views as an integral part of the solution to the problems highlighted by the events of September 11 and the aftermath.
- In the first lesson, educators introduce students to the "Believing Game," encouraging students to identify with feelings, thoughts and beliefs of a person with views different than their own.
- In the second lesson, students are asked to identify civil rights and liberties and discuss how integral these principles are to defining what it means to be an American. Educators present students with a list of events that have occurred in the United States prior to and after September 11. Students are asked to reflect upon their feelings about the events, and share their feelings with the class. Educators facilitate and encourage students to understand that there are different perspectives other than their own, and consider the extent to which the values and concerns presented have a common link.

Objectives of activity:
Students will:
- examine their conflicting thoughts regarding the events of September 11 and the aftermath;
- hear and discuss the thoughts of their peers;
- critically read articles that present differing views on an issue;
- discuss the positive and negative aspects of maintaining democracy in difficult times;
- look for fears/longings/needs/interests that drive differing views;
- respect different viewpoints by analyzing and understanding them; and
- practice perspective-taking by putting themselves in the shoes of others.

Subjects with which this lesson interfaces:
Language Arts, History, Civics

Estimated time of activity:
Two 45-50 minute class periods, and 20 minutes of prior background reading as homework

National educational standards that this lesson meets:
• McRel: Standards for Civics
• McRel: Standards for History
• McRel: Standards for Language Arts

** This complete lesson plan is available for free at www.911AsHistory.org. The "Re-Examining Democracy in a Post September 11 World" lesson plan, including a list of required materials and detailed teaching procedure with assessment recommendations and extended activities, downloads as a 15-page document.

Reflect, Reach Out, Rebuild... Creating a Commemorative Time Capsule

Do Something, Inc.

Themes covered:
Helping Children Find and Give Support within their Communities
Helping Children Identify and Respect American Values

Overview of activity:
Through the creation of a time capsule, students will explore themes of citizenship and values as shaped by the events of September 11.

- In the first lesson, students explore what being an American means to them, and develop a list of themes that reflect the most significant values in their lives, community and nation. The concept and definition of a time capsule is then discussed, and students are encouraged to understand how the items placed in time capsules reflect the values and themes of their times.

- In the second lesson, students break into small groups, and using the themes created in the first lesson, develop lists of potential objects, items or images for their own time capsule that reflect their ideals and values.

- In the third lesson, educators facilitate discussions with students on time capsule details, such as when it should be opened and where it should be stored. Students present to the class their suggestions of items to be included, and using a group decision-making activity, the class selects the contents to be placed in the time capsule. Educators explore with students whether the items selected reflect what America means to them, and how their values would be imparted to those who open the time capsule in the future.

Objectives of activity:
Students will:
- develop a deeper understanding and appreciation of what it means to be both an American and an active citizen;
- gain an appreciation of the values that define themselves and their communities; and
- share what they learn with the larger community.

Subjects with which this lesson interfaces:
History, English, Language Arts, Civics, Social Studies

Estimated time of activity:
Two to three class periods (plus additional homework assignment)

National educational standards that this lesson meets:
• McRel: Standards for Civics
• McRel: Standards for History
• McRel: Standards for Language Arts

** This complete lesson plan is available for free at www.911AsHistory.org.
The "Reflect, Reach Out, Rebuild… Creating a Commemorative Time
Capsule" lesson plan, including a list of required materials and detailed
teaching procedure with assessment recommendations and extended activities, downloads as a 15-page document.

ACKNOWLEDGEMENTS

9/11 As History Advisory Board:

George Burns, Principal, Ethical Culture Fieldston Lower School, Bronx, New York

Dr. Suzanne Carothers, Professor, Steinhardt School of Education, Department of Teaching and Learning, New York University, New York, New York

Jill Cook, Director of Programs, American School Counselor Association, Alexandria, Virginia

Tim Devine, 11th Grade Teacher, Northside College Preparatory High School, Chicago, Illinois

Whitney Finn, 7th Grade Teacher, Bedford Middle School, Westport, Connecticut

Frank Hogan, Headmaster, The Latin School of Chicago, Chicago, Illinois

Dr. Paul Houston, Executive Director, American Association of School Administrators, Arlington, Virginia

Tom Kelchner, Principal, Marsh Middle School, Dallas, Texas; President, Dallas School Administrator's Association

John Love, Vice President for Academic Affairs, The Latin School of Chicago, Chicago, Illinois

Marcello Mongardi, Pre-K/Kindergarten Teacher, Children's Workshop, New York, New York

James McGrath Morris, 12th Grade Government Teacher, West Springfield High School, Springfield, Virginia

Teresa Pless, 2nd Grade Teacher, Smiths Station Elementary School, Smiths Station, Alabama

Nicole Yohalem, Manager of Learning and Research, Forum for Youth Investment, Takoma Park, Maryland

Lesson Plan and Other Developers:

Anti-Defamation League (http://www.adl.org)

Do Something, Inc.

Educators for Social Responsibility (http://www.esrnational.org)

National Institute on Media and the Family (http://www.mediafamily.org)

Post September 11 Education Consortium (http://www.911edconsortium.org/)

Reading Rainbow (http://gpn.unl.edu/rainbow/)

Whitney Finn, 7th Grade Teacher, Bedford Middle School

Robin Gurwitch, PhD, University of Oklahoma Health Sciences Center

Virginia Kimball, Volunteer, The American Red Cross

James McGrath Morris, 12th Grade Government Teacher, West Springfield High School

Kathleen Anderson Steeves, PhD, George Washington University

Maureen Underwood, MSW, LCSW, Coordinator, Families GOALS Project

9/11: Looking Back, Moving Forward

Design: **Froeter Design Company, Inc.**
(http://www.froeterdesign.com)

Artwork Contributions: **Conflict Resolution Center of West Shore, Inc.**, Westlake, Ohio
SHiNE (http://www.shine.com)

Ellen Galinsky, President

Lois Backon, *9/11 As History* Project Director

Erin Brownfield, Director of Communications

Kelly Sakai, Communications and Program Associate

Kimberlee Salmond, former Research Associate

Families and Work Institute and Bank One launched the *9/11 As History* Web site in the summer of 2002. By the date of this book's printing, more than 5,000 students have written in, sharing their thoughts and feelings. This book features a selection of those writings, in addition to artwork from students. These were chosen to reflect the full range of views and thoughts expressed and provide a poignant glimpse into young people's opinions about September 11 as well how these attacks changed them, their communities, the nation and the world.

We encourage educators to tell students about the *9/11 As History* Web site and invite them to contribute to the student writing section so that all of us can continue to listen and learn from our nation's youth.

In addition, the Web site, www.911AsHistory.org contains many practical and useful resources for adults in Spanish and English, including tips for parents and educators, suggested reading lists and other links and activities. We thank the students and educators of America and the organizations and individuals who worked with us for their contributions to *9/11 As History*.

For more information on ordering copies of *9/11: Looking Back, Moving Forward*, please visit www.911AsHistory.org

Familiesand**Work**Institute